PRODUCTIVITY JOURNAL

For the Productivity Oriented Muslim

Towards becoming Muhsin

IHSAN JOURNALS

IHSAN JOURNALS

For the Productivity Oriented Muslim

İhsan Planner

A step towards becoming Muhsin

This planner belongs to

Name ______________________________

Phone ______________________________

Email ______________________________

Create your mission statement

____

____

____

____

Take advantage of **FIVE** before **FIVE:**
your **YOUTH** before your **OLD AGE,**
your **HEALTH** before your **ILLNESS,**
your **RICHES** before your **POVERTY,**
your **FREE TIME** before your **WORK,**
and your **LIFE** before your **DEATH.**

– Messenger of Allah (PBUH)

Keeping Promises

**Verily,
the covenant will
be questioned.**

[TMQ Surah Al-Isra : 34]

NIYYAH - MONTHLY PLANNING

What do I hope to accomplish by the month's end? Why?

What are the benefits & drawbacks of my goals/intentions?

What must I do in order to carry out my intentions?

What challenges have I faced? How can I overcome these challenges?

NIYYAH - WEEKLY PLANNING

WEEKLY GOALS

1.
2.
3.
4.

WEEKLY TASKS

"If you are grateful, I will add more (favours) unto you."
(Quran 14:7)

THINGS I THANK ALLAH ﷻ FOR	WHAT I LEARNED

DAILY PLANNING & REFLECTION

What vital goals do you have for today?

List your top 5 priorities for today,
ensuring they align with your weekly goals.

1. ______
2. ______
3. ______
4. ______
5. ______

What will you make dua or offer istikharah for today?

Today's Reflection

DAILY PLANNING & REFLECTION

What vital goals do you have for today?

List your top 5 priorities for today, ensuring they align with your weekly goals.

1. ______
2. ______
3. ______
4. ______
5. ______

What will you make dua or offer istikharah for today?

______

______

______

______

______

Today's Reflection

______

______

______

______

______

______

______

______

DAILY PLANNING & REFLECTION

What vital goals do you have for today?

List your top 5 priorities for today,
ensuring they align with your weekly goals.

1. ____________________
2. ____________________
3. ____________________
4. ____________________
5. ____________________

What will you make dua or offer istikharah for today?

Today's Reflection

DAILY PLANNING & REFLECTION

What vital goals do you have for today?

List your top 5 priorities for today, ensuring they align with your weekly goals.

1. ______________________________
2. ______________________________
3. ______________________________
4. ______________________________
5. ______________________________

What will you make dua or offer istikharah for today?

Today's Reflection

DAILY PLANNING & REFLECTION

What vital goals do you have for today?

List your top 5 priorities for today,
ensuring they align with your weekly goals.

1. ______________________________
2. ______________________________
3. ______________________________
4. ______________________________
5. ______________________________

What will you make dua or offer istikharah for today?

Today's Reflection

DAILY PLANNING & REFLECTION

What vital goals do you have for today?

List your top 5 priorities for today, ensuring they align with your weekly goals.

1. ____________________
2. ____________________
3. ____________________
4. ____________________
5. ____________________

What will you make dua or offer istikharah for today?

Today's Reflection

DAILY PLANNING & REFLECTION

What vital goals do you have for today?

List your top 5 priorities for today,
ensuring they align with your weekly goals.

1. ______________________________
2. ______________________________
3. ______________________________
4. ______________________________
5. ______________________________

What will you make dua or offer istikharah for today?

____

____

____

____

____

Today's Reflection

____

____

____

____

____

____

____

____

MUHASABA - WEEKLY REVIEW

For what do you feel thankful to Allah ﷻ this week?

Which goals did you manage to concentrate on this week?

What have you discovered this week about yourself or your intentions?

What do you plan to prioritise for the coming week?

What instances or stories of Barakah did you have this week?

NIYYAH - WEEKLY PLANNING

WEEKLY GOALS

1.
2.
3.
4.

WEEKLY TASKS

"If you are grateful, I will add more (favours) unto you."
(Quran 14:7)

THINGS I THANK ALLAH ﷻ FOR	WHAT I LEARNED

DAILY PLANNING & REFLECTION

What vital goals do you have for today?

List your top 5 priorities for today, ensuring they align with your weekly goals.

1. ____________________
2. ____________________
3. ____________________
4. ____________________
5. ____________________

What will you make dua or offer istikharah for today?

Today's Reflection

DAILY PLANNING & REFLECTION

What vital goals do you have for today?

List your top 5 priorities for today,
ensuring they align with your weekly goals.

1. ________________________

2. ________________________

3. ________________________

4. ________________________

5. ________________________

What will you make dua or offer istikharah for today?

Today's Reflection

DAILY PLANNING & REFLECTION

What vital goals do you have for today?

List your top 5 priorities for today, ensuring they align with your weekly goals.

1. ____________________
2. ____________________
3. ____________________
4. ____________________
5. ____________________

What will you make dua or offer istikharah for today?

Today's Reflection

DAILY PLANNING & REFLECTION

What vital goals do you have for today?

List your top 5 priorities for today,
ensuring they align with your weekly goals.

1. ______________________________
2. ______________________________
3. ______________________________
4. ______________________________
5. ______________________________

What will you make dua or offer istikharah for today?

____
____
____
____
____

Today's Reflection

____
____
____
____
____
____
____
____

DAILY PLANNING & REFLECTION

What vital goals do you have for today?

List your top 5 priorities for today, ensuring they align with your weekly goals.

1. ____________________
2. ____________________
3. ____________________
4. ____________________
5. ____________________

What will you make dua or offer istikharah for today?

Today's Reflection

DAILY PLANNING & REFLECTION

What vital goals do you have for today?

List your top 5 priorities for today,
ensuring they align with your weekly goals.

1. ______
2. ______
3. ______
4. ______
5. ______

What will you make dua or offer istikharah for today?

Today's Reflection

DAILY PLANNING & REFLECTION

What vital goals do you have for today?

List your top 5 priorities for today, ensuring they align with your weekly goals.

1. ____________________________
2. ____________________________
3. ____________________________
4. ____________________________
5. ____________________________

What will you make dua or offer istikharah for today?

Today's Reflection

MUHASABA - WEEKLY REVIEW

For what do you feel thankful to Allah ﷻ this week?

Which goals did you manage to concentrate on this week?

What have you discovered this week about yourself or your intentions?

What do you plan to prioritise for the coming week?

What instances or stories of Barakah did you have this week?

NIYYAH - WEEKLY PLANNING

WEEKLY GOALS
1.
2.
3.
4.

WEEKLY TASKS	

"If you are grateful, I will add more (favours) unto you."
(Quran 14:7)

THINGS I THANK ALLAH ﷻ FOR	WHAT I LEARNED

DAILY PLANNING & REFLECTION

What vital goals do you have for today?

List your top 5 priorities for today,
ensuring they align with your weekly goals.

1. ______________________________
2. ______________________________
3. ______________________________
4. ______________________________
5. ______________________________

What will you make dua or offer istikharah for today?

____
____
____
____
____

Today's Reflection

____
____
____
____
____
____
____
____

DAILY PLANNING & REFLECTION

What vital goals do you have for today?

List your top 5 priorities for today, ensuring they align with your weekly goals.

1. ______________________
2. ______________________
3. ______________________
4. ______________________
5. ______________________

What will you make dua or offer istikharah for today?

____

____

____

____

____

Today's Reflection

____

____

____

____

____

____

____

____

DAILY PLANNING & REFLECTION

What vital goals do you have for today?

List your top 5 priorities for today,
ensuring they align with your weekly goals.

1. ______________________________
2. ______________________________
3. ______________________________
4. ______________________________
5. ______________________________

What will you make dua or offer Istikharah for today?

Today's Reflection

DAILY PLANNING & REFLECTION

What vital goals do you have for today?

List your top 5 priorities for today, ensuring they align with your weekly goals.

1. ____________________
2. ____________________
3. ____________________
4. ____________________
5. ____________________

What will you make dua or offer istikharah for today?

____
____
____
____
____

Today's Reflection

____
____
____
____
____
____
____
____

DAILY PLANNING & REFLECTION

What vital goals do you have for today?

List your top 5 priorities for today,
ensuring they align with your weekly goals.

1. ______________________________
2. ______________________________
3. ______________________________
4. ______________________________
5. ______________________________

What will you make dua or offer istikharah for today?

Today's Reflection

DAILY PLANNING & REFLECTION

What vital goals do you have for today?

List your top 5 priorities for today, ensuring they align with your weekly goals.

1. ______________________
2. ______________________
3. ______________________
4. ______________________
5. ______________________

What will you make dua or offer istikharah for today?

____

____

____

____

____

Today's Reflection

____

____

____

____

____

____

____

____

DAILY PLANNING & REFLECTION

What vital goals do you have for today?

List your top 5 priorities for today,
ensuring they align with your weekly goals.

1. ____________________
2. ____________________
3. ____________________
4. ____________________
5. ____________________

What will you make dua or offer istikharah for today?

____
____
____
____
____

Today's Reflection

____
____
____
____
____
____
____
____

MUHASABA - WEEKLY REVIEW

For what do you feel thankful to Allah ﷻ this week?

Which goals did you manage to concentrate on this week?

What have you discovered this week about yourself or your intentions?

What do you plan to prioritise for the coming week?

What instances or stories of Barakah did you have this week?

NIYYAH - WEEKLY PLANNING

WEEKLY GOALS

1.
2.
3.
4.

WEEKLY TASKS

"If you are grateful, I will add more (favours) unto you."
(Quran 14:7)

THINGS I THANK ALLAH ﷻ FOR	WHAT I LEARNED

DAILY PLANNING & REFLECTION

What vital goals do you have for today?

List your top 5 priorities for today, ensuring they align with your weekly goals.

1. ______
2. ______
3. ______
4. ______
5. ______

What will you make dua or offer istikharah for today?

______

______

______

______

______

Today's Reflection

______

______

______

______

______

______

______

______

DAILY PLANNING & REFLECTION

What vital goals do you have for today?

List your top 5 priorities for today,
ensuring they align with your weekly goals.

1. ____

2. ____

3. ____

4. ____

5. ____

What will you make dua or offer istikharah for today?

Today's Reflection

DAILY PLANNING & REFLECTION

What vital goals do you have for today?

List your top 5 priorities for today,
ensuring they align with your weekly goals.

1. ____________________
2. ____________________
3. ____________________
4. ____________________
5. ____________________

What will you make dua or offer istikharah for today?

____

____

____

____

____

Today's Reflection

____

____

____

____

____

____

____

____

DAILY PLANNING & REFLECTION

What vital goals do you have for today?

List your top 5 priorities for today,
ensuring they align with your weekly goals.

1. ______
2. ______
3. ______
4. ______
5. ______

What will you make dua or offer istikharah for today?

Today's Reflection

DAILY PLANNING & REFLECTION

What vital goals do you have for today?

List your top 5 priorities for today, ensuring they align with your weekly goals.

1. ______________________________
2. ______________________________
3. ______________________________
4. ______________________________
5. ______________________________

What will you make dua or offer istikharah for today?

____

____

____

____

____

Today's Reflection

____

____

____

____

____

____

____

____

DAILY PLANNING & REFLECTION

What vital goals do you have for today?

List your top 5 priorities for today,
ensuring they align with your weekly goals.

1. ______________________________
2. ______________________________
3. ______________________________
4. ______________________________
5. ______________________________

What will you make dua or offer istikharah for today?

Today's Reflection

DAILY PLANNING & REFLECTION

What vital goals do you have for today?

List your top 5 priorities for today, ensuring they align with your weekly goals.

1. ______
2. ______
3. ______
4. ______
5. ______

What will you make dua or offer istikharah for today?

______

______

______

______

______

Today's Reflection

______

______

______

______

______

______

______

______

MUHASABA - WEEKLY REVIEW

For what do you feel thankful to Allah ﷻ this week?

Which goals did you manage to concentrate on this week?

What have you discovered this week about yourself or your intentions?

What do you plan to prioritise for the coming week?

What instances or stories of Barakah did you have this week?

MUHASABA - MONTHLY REVIEW

What did I accomplish? What did I fail to accomplish?

What benefits & drawbacks have I experienced?

What challenges have I faced? What solutions could I have adopted?

What have I learnt during the last month? How can I improve?

Always Speak the Truth

O you who have believed, fear Allah and speak words of appropriate justice. He will [then] amend for you your deeds and forgive you your sins. And whoever obeys Allah and His Messenger has certainly attained a great attainment.

[TMQ Surah Al-Ahzab : 70-71]

NIYYAH - MONTHLY PLANNING

What do I hope to accomplish by the month's end? Why?

What are the benefits & drawbacks of my goals/intentions?

What must I do in order to carry out my intentions?

What challenges have I faced? How can I overcome these challenges?

NIYYAH - WEEKLY PLANNING

WEEKLY GOALS

1.
2.
3.
4.

WEEKLY TASKS

"If you are grateful, I will add more (favours) unto you."
(Quran 14:7)

THINGS I THANK ALLAH ﷻ FOR	WHAT I LEARNED

DAILY PLANNING & REFLECTION

What vital goals do you have for today?

List your top 5 priorities for today, ensuring they align with your weekly goals.

1. ______
2. ______
3. ______
4. ______
5. ______

What will you make dua or offer istikharah for today?

______

Today's Reflection

______

DAILY PLANNING & REFLECTION

What vital goals do you have for today?

List your top 5 priorities for today, ensuring they align with your weekly goals.

1. ______
2. ______
3. ______
4. ______
5. ______

What will you make dua or offer istikharah for today?

______

______

______

______

______

Today's Reflection

______

______

______

______

______

______

______

______

DAILY PLANNING & REFLECTION

What vital goals do you have for today?

List your top 5 priorities for today,
ensuring they align with your weekly goals.

1. ______________________________

2. ______________________________

3. ______________________________

4. ______________________________

5. ______________________________

What will you make dua or offer Istikharah for today?

Today's Reflection

DAILY PLANNING & REFLECTION

What vital goals do you have for today?

List your top 5 priorities for today, ensuring they align with your weekly goals.

1. ______________________
2. ______________________
3. ______________________
4. ______________________
5. ______________________

What will you make dua or offer istikharah for today?

____

____

____

____

____

Today's Reflection

____

____

____

____

____

____

____

____

DAILY PLANNING & REFLECTION

What vital goals do you have for today?

List your top 5 priorities for today,
ensuring they align with your weekly goals.

1. ______
2. ______
3. ______
4. ______
5. ______

What will you make dua or offer istikharah for today?

Today's Reflection

DAILY PLANNING & REFLECTION

What vital goals do you have for today?

List your top 5 priorities for today, ensuring they align with your weekly goals.

1. ________________________________
2. ________________________________
3. ________________________________
4. ________________________________
5. ________________________________

What will you make dua or offer istikharah for today?

Today's Reflection

DAILY PLANNING & REFLECTION

What vital goals do you have for today?

List your top 5 priorities for today,
ensuring they align with your weekly goals.

1. ______________________________
2. ______________________________
3. ______________________________
4. ______________________________
5. ______________________________

What will you make dua or offer istikharah for today?

____
____
____
____
____

Today's Reflection

____
____
____
____
____
____
____
____

MUHASABA - WEEKLY REVIEW

For what do you feel thankful to Allah ﷻ this week?
Which goals did you manage to concentrate on this week?
What have you discovered this week about yourself or your intentions?
What do you plan to prioritise for the coming week?
What instances or stories of Barakah did you have this week?

NIYYAH - WEEKLY PLANNING

WEEKLY GOALS

1.
2.
3.
4.

WEEKLY TASKS

"If you are grateful, I will add more (favours) unto you."
(Quran 14:7)

THINGS I THANK ALLAH ﷻ FOR	WHAT I LEARNED

DAILY PLANNING & REFLECTION

What vital goals do you have for today?

List your top 5 priorities for today, ensuring they align with your weekly goals.

1. ____________________
2. ____________________
3. ____________________
4. ____________________
5. ____________________

What will you make dua or offer istikharah for today?

____

____

____

____

____

Today's Reflection

____

____

____

____

____

____

____

____

DAILY PLANNING & REFLECTION

What vital goals do you have for today?

List your top 5 priorities for today,
ensuring they align with your weekly goals.

1. ______
2. ______
3. ______
4. ______
5. ______

What will you make dua or offer istikharah for today?

______

______

______

______

______

Today's Reflection

______

______

______

______

______

______

______

______

DAILY PLANNING & REFLECTION

What vital goals do you have for today?

List your top 5 priorities for today, ensuring they align with your weekly goals.

1. ____
2. ____
3. ____
4. ____
5. ____

What will you make dua or offer istikharah for today?

Today's Reflection

DAILY PLANNING & REFLECTION

What vital goals do you have for today?

List your top 5 priorities for today,
ensuring they align with your weekly goals.

1. ____________________
2. ____________________
3. ____________________
4. ____________________
5. ____________________

What will you make dua or offer istikharah for today?

Today's Reflection

DAILY PLANNING & REFLECTION

What vital goals do you have for today?

List your top 5 priorities for today,
ensuring they align with your weekly goals.

1. ______
2. ______
3. ______
4. ______
5. ______

What will you make dua or offer istikharah for today?

Today's Reflection

DAILY PLANNING & REFLECTION

What vital goals do you have for today?

List your top 5 priorities for today,
ensuring they align with your weekly goals.

1. ______
2. ______
3. ______
4. ______
5. ______

What will you make dua or offer istikharah for today?

Today's Reflection

DAILY PLANNING & REFLECTION

What vital goals do you have for today?

List your top 5 priorities for today, ensuring they align with your weekly goals.

1. ______
2. ______
3. ______
4. ______
5. ______

What will you make dua or offer istikharah for today?

Today's Reflection

MUHASABA - WEEKLY REVIEW

For what do you feel thankful to Allah ﷻ this week?

Which goals did you manage to concentrate on this week?

What have you discovered this week about yourself or your intentions?

What do you plan to prioritise for the coming week?

What instances or stories of Barakah did you have this week?

NIYYAH - WEEKLY PLANNING

WEEKLY GOALS

1.
2.
3.
4.

WEEKLY TASKS

"If you are grateful, I will add more (favours) unto you."
(Quran 14:7)

THINGS I THANK ALLAH ﷻ FOR	WHAT I LEARNED

DAILY PLANNING & REFLECTION

What vital goals do you have for today?

List your top 5 priorities for today,
ensuring they align with your weekly goals.

1. ____

2. ____

3. ____

4. ____

5. ____

What will you make dua or offer istikharah for today?

Today's Reflection

DAILY PLANNING & REFLECTION

What vital goals do you have for today?

List your top 5 priorities for today, ensuring they align with your weekly goals.

1. ____________________
2. ____________________
3. ____________________
4. ____________________
5. ____________________

What will you make dua or offer istikharah for today?

Today's Reflection

DAILY PLANNING & REFLECTION

What vital goals do you have for today?

List your top 5 priorities for today,
ensuring they align with your weekly goals.

1. ______________________________
2. ______________________________
3. ______________________________
4. ______________________________
5. ______________________________

What will you make dua or offer istikharah for today?

Today's Reflection

DAILY PLANNING & REFLECTION

What vital goals do you have for today?

List your top 5 priorities for today, ensuring they align with your weekly goals.

1. ________________________________
2. ________________________________
3. ________________________________
4. ________________________________
5. ________________________________

What will you make dua or offer istikharah for today?

Today's Reflection

DAILY PLANNING & REFLECTION

What vital goals do you have for today?

List your top 5 priorities for today,
ensuring they align with your weekly goals.

1. ______
2. ______
3. ______
4. ______
5. ______

What will you make dua or offer istikharah for today?

______

______

______

______

______

Today's Reflection

______

______

______

______

______

______

______

______

DAILY PLANNING & REFLECTION

What vital goals do you have for today?

List your top 5 priorities for today,
ensuring they align with your weekly goals.

1. ____________________
2. ____________________
3. ____________________
4. ____________________
5. ____________________

What will you make dua or offer istikharah for today?

____

____

____

____

____

Today's Reflection

____

____

____

____

____

____

____

____

DAILY PLANNING & REFLECTION

What vital goals do you have for today?

List your top 5 priorities for today,
ensuring they align with your weekly goals.

1. ______
2. ______
3. ______
4. ______
5. ______

What will you make dua or offer istikharah for today?

______

______

______

______

______

Today's Reflection

______

______

______

______

______

______

______

______

MUHASABA - WEEKLY REVIEW

For what do you feel thankful to Allah ﷻ this week?
Which goals did you manage to concentrate on this week?
What have you discovered this week about yourself or your intentions?
What do you plan to prioritise for the coming week?
What instances or stories of Barakah did you have this week?

NIYYAH - WEEKLY PLANNING

WEEKLY GOALS
1.
2.
3.
4.

WEEKLY TASKS	

"If you are grateful, I will add more (favours) unto you."
(Quran 14:7)

THINGS I THANK ALLAH ﷻ FOR	WHAT I LEARNED

DAILY PLANNING & REFLECTION

What vital goals do you have for today?

**List your top 5 priorities for today,
ensuring they align with your weekly goals.**

1. ______________________________
2. ______________________________
3. ______________________________
4. ______________________________
5. ______________________________

What will you make dua or offer istikharah for today?

____

____

____

____

____

Today's Reflection

____

____

____

____

____

____

____

____

DAILY PLANNING & REFLECTION

What vital goals do you have for today?

List your top 5 priorities for today,
ensuring they align with your weekly goals.

1. ____

2. ____

3. ____

4. ____

5. ____

What will you make dua or offer istikharah for today?

Today's Reflection

DAILY PLANNING & REFLECTION

What vital goals do you have for today?

List your top 5 priorities for today, ensuring they align with your weekly goals.

1. ____________________
2. ____________________
3. ____________________
4. ____________________
5. ____________________

What will you make dua or offer istikharah for today?

Today's Reflection

DAILY PLANNING & REFLECTION

What vital goals do you have for today?

List your top 5 priorities for today, ensuring they align with your weekly goals.

1. ____________________
2. ____________________
3. ____________________
4. ____________________
5. ____________________

What will you make dua or offer istikharah for today?

Today's Reflection

DAILY PLANNING & REFLECTION

What vital goals do you have for today?

List your top 5 priorities for today, ensuring they align with your weekly goals.

1. ______________________
2. ______________________
3. ______________________
4. ______________________
5. ______________________

What will you make dua or offer istikharah for today?

____

____

____

____

____

Today's Reflection

____

____

____

____

____

____

____

____

DAILY PLANNING & REFLECTION

What vital goals do you have for today?

**List your top 5 priorities for today,
ensuring they align with your weekly goals.**

1. ____
2. ____
3. ____
4. ____
5. ____

What will you make dua or offer istikharah for today?

Today's Reflection

DAILY PLANNING & REFLECTION

What vital goals do you have for today?

List your top 5 priorities for today, ensuring they align with your weekly goals.

1. ____
2. ____
3. ____
4. ____
5. ____

What will you make dua or offer istikharah for today?

Today's Reflection

MUHASABA - WEEKLY REVIEW

For what do you feel thankful to Allah ﷻ this week?

Which goals did you manage to concentrate on this week?

What have you discovered this week about yourself or your intentions?

What do you plan to prioritise for the coming week?

What instances or stories of Barakah did you have this week?

MUHASABA - MONTHLY REVIEW

What did I accomplish? What did I fail to accomplish?
What benefits & drawbacks have I experienced?
What challenges have I faced? What solutions could I have adopted?
What have I learnt during the last month? How can I improve?

Manage Your Anger

“

The Messenger of Allah (PBUH) said:

If any of you becomes angry and he is standing, let him sit down, so his anger will go away. If it does not go away, let him lie down.

”

[Abu Dawud, Book No. 034, Hadith No. 4764]

NIYYAH - MONTHLY PLANNING

What do I hope to accomplish by the month's end? Why?

What are the benefits & drawbacks of my goals/intentions?

What must I do in order to carry out my intentions?

What challenges have I faced? How can I overcome these challenges?

NIYYAH - WEEKLY PLANNING

WEEKLY GOALS

1.
2.
3.
4.

WEEKLY TASKS

"If you are grateful, I will add more (favours) unto you."
(Quran 14:7)

THINGS I THANK ALLAH ﷻ FOR	WHAT I LEARNED

DAILY PLANNING & REFLECTION

What vital goals do you have for today?

List your top 5 priorities for today, ensuring they align with your weekly goals.

1. ______
2. ______
3. ______
4. ______
5. ______

What will you make dua or offer istikharah for today?

______

______

______

______

______

Today's Reflection

______

______

______

______

______

______

______

______

DAILY PLANNING & REFLECTION

What vital goals do you have for today?

List your top 5 priorities for today, ensuring they align with your weekly goals.

1. ________________________________
2. ________________________________
3. ________________________________
4. ________________________________
5. ________________________________

What will you make dua or offer istikharah for today?

Today's Reflection

DAILY PLANNING & REFLECTION

What vital goals do you have for today?

List your top 5 priorities for today, ensuring they align with your weekly goals.

1. ______________________________
2. ______________________________
3. ______________________________
4. ______________________________
5. ______________________________

What will you make dua or offer istikharah for today?

____

____

____

____

____

Today's Reflection

____

____

____

____

____

____

____

____

DAILY PLANNING & REFLECTION

What vital goals do you have for today?

List your top 5 priorities for today, ensuring they align with your weekly goals.

1. ______
2. ______
3. ______
4. ______
5. ______

What will you make dua or offer istikharah for today?

Today's Reflection

DAILY PLANNING & REFLECTION

What vital goals do you have for today?

List your top 5 priorities for today,
ensuring they align with your weekly goals.

1. ____
2. ____
3. ____
4. ____
5. ____

What will you make dua or offer istikharah for today?

Today's Reflection

DAILY PLANNING & REFLECTION

What vital goals do you have for today?

List your top 5 priorities for today, ensuring they align with your weekly goals.

1. ______________________
2. ______________________
3. ______________________
4. ______________________
5. ______________________

What will you make dua or offer istikharah for today?

____

____

____

____

____

Today's Reflection

____

____

____

____

____

____

____

____

DAILY PLANNING & REFLECTION

What vital goals do you have for today?

List your top 5 priorities for today, ensuring they align with your weekly goals.

1. ____________________
2. ____________________
3. ____________________
4. ____________________
5. ____________________

What will you make dua or offer istikharah for today?

____

____

____

____

____

Today's Reflection

____

____

____

____

____

____

____

____

MUHASABA - WEEKLY REVIEW

For what do you feel thankful to Allah ﷻ this week?
Which goals did you manage to concentrate on this week?
What have you discovered this week about yourself or your intentions?
What do you plan to prioritise for the coming week?
What instances or stories of Barakah did you have this week?

NIYYAH - WEEKLY PLANNING

WEEKLY GOALS

1.
2.
3.
4.

WEEKLY TASKS

"If you are grateful, I will add more (favours) unto you."
(Quran 14:7)

THINGS I THANK ALLAH ﷻ FOR	WHAT I LEARNED

DAILY PLANNING & REFLECTION

What vital goals do you have for today?

List your top 5 priorities for today, ensuring they align with your weekly goals.

1. __________
2. __________
3. __________
4. __________
5. __________

What will you make dua or offer istikharah for today?

Today's Reflection

DAILY PLANNING & REFLECTION

What vital goals do you have for today?

List your top 5 priorities for today,
ensuring they align with your weekly goals.

1. ____________________
2. ____________________
3. ____________________
4. ____________________
5. ____________________

What will you make dua or offer istikharah for today?

Today's Reflection

DAILY PLANNING & REFLECTION

What vital goals do you have for today?

List your top 5 priorities for today, ensuring they align with your weekly goals.

1. ____________________
2. ____________________
3. ____________________
4. ____________________
5. ____________________

What will you make dua or offer istikharah for today?

____
____
____
____
____

Today's Reflection

____
____
____
____
____
____
____
____

DAILY PLANNING & REFLECTION

What vital goals do you have for today?

List your top 5 priorities for today,
ensuring they align with your weekly goals.

1. ______________________________
2. ______________________________
3. ______________________________
4. ______________________________
5. ______________________________

What will you make dua or offer Istikharah for today?

____

____

____

____

____

Today's Reflection

____

____

____

____

____

____

____

____

DAILY PLANNING & REFLECTION

What vital goals do you have for today?

List your top 5 priorities for today, ensuring they align with your weekly goals.

1. ____________________
2. ____________________
3. ____________________
4. ____________________
5. ____________________

What will you make dua or offer istikharah for today?

Today's Reflection

DAILY PLANNING & REFLECTION

What vital goals do you have for today?

List your top 5 priorities for today, ensuring they align with your weekly goals.

1. ____________________
2. ____________________
3. ____________________
4. ____________________
5. ____________________

What will you make dua or offer istikharah for today?

Today's Reflection

DAILY PLANNING & REFLECTION

What vital goals do you have for today?

List your top 5 priorities for today, ensuring they align with your weekly goals.

1. ____________________
2. ____________________
3. ____________________
4. ____________________
5. ____________________

What will you make dua or offer istikharah for today?

Today's Reflection

MUHASABA - WEEKLY REVIEW

For what do you feel thankful to Allah ﷻ this week?

Which goals did you manage to concentrate on this week?

What have you discovered this week about yourself or your intentions?

What do you plan to prioritise for the coming week?

What instances or stories of Barakah did you have this week?

NIYYAH - WEEKLY PLANNING

WEEKLY GOALS

1.
2.
3.
4.

WEEKLY TASKS

"If you are grateful, I will add more (favours) unto you."
(Quran 14:7)

THINGS I THANK ALLAH ﷻ FOR	WHAT I LEARNED

DAILY PLANNING & REFLECTION

What vital goals do you have for today?

List your top 5 priorities for today,
ensuring they align with your weekly goals.

1. ____________________
2. ____________________
3. ____________________
4. ____________________
5. ____________________

What will you make dua or offer Istikharah for today?

Today's Reflection

DAILY PLANNING & REFLECTION

What vital goals do you have for today?

**List your top 5 priorities for today,
ensuring they align with your weekly goals.**

1. ______________________________
2. ______________________________
3. ______________________________
4. ______________________________
5. ______________________________

What will you make dua or offer istikharah for today?

____
____
____
____
____

Today's Reflection

____
____
____
____
____
____
____
____

DAILY PLANNING & REFLECTION

What vital goals do you have for today?

List your top 5 priorities for today, ensuring they align with your weekly goals.

1. __________
2. __________
3. __________
4. __________
5. __________

What will you make dua or offer istikharah for today?

Today's Reflection

DAILY PLANNING & REFLECTION

What vital goals do you have for today?

List your top 5 priorities for today,
ensuring they align with your weekly goals.

1. ______________________________
2. ______________________________
3. ______________________________
4. ______________________________
5. ______________________________

What will you make dua or offer istikharah for today?

____
____
____
____
____

Today's Reflection

____
____
____
____
____
____
____
____

DAILY PLANNING & REFLECTION

What vital goals do you have for today?

List your top 5 priorities for today, ensuring they align with your weekly goals.

1. ______________________________
2. ______________________________
3. ______________________________
4. ______________________________
5. ______________________________

What will you make dua or offer istikharah for today?

Today's Reflection

DAILY PLANNING & REFLECTION

What vital goals do you have for today?

List your top 5 priorities for today, ensuring they align with your weekly goals.

1. ______
2. ______
3. ______
4. ______
5. ______

What will you make dua or offer istikharah for today?

______

______

______

______

______

Today's Reflection

______

______

______

______

______

______

______

______

DAILY PLANNING & REFLECTION

What vital goals do you have for today?

List your top 5 priorities for today,
ensuring they align with your weekly goals.

1. ______
2. ______
3. ______
4. ______
5. ______

What will you make dua or offer istikharah for today?

Today's Reflection

MUHASABA - WEEKLY REVIEW

For what do you feel thankful to Allah ﷻ this week?

Which goals did you manage to concentrate on this week?

What have you discovered this week about yourself or your intentions?

What do you plan to prioritise for the coming week?

What instances or stories of Barakah did you have this week?

NIYYAH - WEEKLY PLANNING

WEEKLY GOALS

1.
2.
3.
4.

WEEKLY TASKS

"If you are grateful, I will add more (favours) unto you."
(Quran 14:7)

THINGS I THANK ALLAH ﷻ FOR	WHAT I LEARNED

DAILY PLANNING & REFLECTION

What vital goals do you have for today?

List your top 5 priorities for today, ensuring they align with your weekly goals.

1. ____________________
2. ____________________
3. ____________________
4. ____________________
5. ____________________

What will you make dua or offer istikharah for today?

Today's Reflection

DAILY PLANNING & REFLECTION

What vital goals do you have for today?

List your top 5 priorities for today,
ensuring they align with your weekly goals.

1. ______________________________

2. ______________________________

3. ______________________________

4. ______________________________

5. ______________________________

What will you make dua or offer istikharah for today?

Today's Reflection

DAILY PLANNING & REFLECTION

What vital goals do you have for today?

List your top 5 priorities for today, ensuring they align with your weekly goals.

1. ____________________
2. ____________________
3. ____________________
4. ____________________
5. ____________________

What will you make dua or offer istikharah for today?

____
____
____
____
____

Today's Reflection

____
____
____
____
____
____
____
____

DAILY PLANNING & REFLECTION

What vital goals do you have for today?

List your top 5 priorities for today, ensuring they align with your weekly goals.

1. ____________________
2. ____________________
3. ____________________
4. ____________________
5. ____________________

What will you make dua or offer istikharah for today?

Today's Reflection

DAILY PLANNING & REFLECTION

What vital goals do you have for today?

List your top 5 priorities for today, ensuring they align with your weekly goals.

1. ______
2. ______
3. ______
4. ______
5. ______

What will you make dua or offer istikharah for today?

______

Today's Reflection

______

DAILY PLANNING & REFLECTION

What vital goals do you have for today?

List your top 5 priorities for today,
ensuring they align with your weekly goals.

1. ______________________________
2. ______________________________
3. ______________________________
4. ______________________________
5. ______________________________

What will you make dua or offer istikharah for today?

____
____
____
____
____

Today's Reflection

____
____
____
____
____
____
____
____

DAILY PLANNING & REFLECTION

What vital goals do you have for today?

List your top 5 priorities for today, ensuring they align with your weekly goals.

1. ______________________________
2. ______________________________
3. ______________________________
4. ______________________________
5. ______________________________

What will you make dua or offer istikharah for today?

Today's Reflection

MUHASABA - WEEKLY REVIEW

For what do you feel thankful to Allah ﷻ this week?
Which goals did you manage to concentrate on this week?
What have you discovered this week about yourself or your intentions?
What do you plan to prioritise for the coming week?
What instances or stories of Barakah did you have this week?

MUHASABA - MONTHLY REVIEW

What did I accomplish? What did I fail to accomplish?

What benefits & drawbacks have I experienced?

What challenges have I faced? What solutions could I have adopted?

What have I learnt during the last month? How can I improve?

Show Respect

The Messenger of Allah (PBUH) said:

He does not belong to us who does not show mercy to our young ones and respect to our old ones, who does not recommend what is reputable and prohibit what is disreputable

[Tirmidhi]

NIYYAH - MONTHLY PLANNING

What do I hope to accomplish by the month's end? Why?

What are the benefits & drawbacks of my goals/intentions?

What must I do in order to carry out my intentions?

What challenges have I faced? How can I overcome these challenges?

NIYYAH - WEEKLY PLANNING

WEEKLY GOALS

1.
2.
3.
4.

WEEKLY TASKS

"If you are grateful, I will add more (favours) unto you."
(Quran 14:7)

THINGS I THANK ALLAH ﷻ FOR	WHAT I LEARNED

DAILY PLANNING & REFLECTION

What vital goals do you have for today?

List your top 5 priorities for today, ensuring they align with your weekly goals.

1. ____________________
2. ____________________
3. ____________________
4. ____________________
5. ____________________

What will you make dua or offer istikharah for today?

Today's Reflection

DAILY PLANNING & REFLECTION

What vital goals do you have for today?

List your top 5 priorities for today, ensuring they align with your weekly goals.

1. ____________________
2. ____________________
3. ____________________
4. ____________________
5. ____________________

What will you make dua or offer istikharah for today?

____

____

____

____

____

Today's Reflection

____

____

____

____

____

____

____

____

DAILY PLANNING & REFLECTION

What vital goals do you have for today?

List your top 5 priorities for today,
ensuring they align with your weekly goals.

1. ____________________

2. ____________________

3. ____________________

4. ____________________

5. ____________________

What will you make dua or offer istikharah for today?

Today's Reflection

DAILY PLANNING & REFLECTION

What vital goals do you have for today?

List your top 5 priorities for today, ensuring they align with your weekly goals.

1. ______
2. ______
3. ______
4. ______
5. ______

What will you make dua or offer istikharah for today?

______

Today's Reflection

______

DAILY PLANNING & REFLECTION

What vital goals do you have for today?

List your top 5 priorities for today,
ensuring they align with your weekly goals.

1. ______________________________
2. ______________________________
3. ______________________________
4. ______________________________
5. ______________________________

What will you make dua or offer istikharah for today?

Today's Reflection

DAILY PLANNING & REFLECTION

What vital goals do you have for today?

List your top 5 priorities for today, ensuring they align with your weekly goals.

1. ____________________
2. ____________________
3. ____________________
4. ____________________
5. ____________________

What will you make dua or offer istikharah for today?

Today's Reflection

DAILY PLANNING & REFLECTION

What vital goals do you have for today?

List your top 5 priorities for today, ensuring they align with your weekly goals.

1. ____________________
2. ____________________
3. ____________________
4. ____________________
5. ____________________

What will you make dua or offer istikharah for today?

Today's Reflection

MUHASABA - WEEKLY REVIEW

For what do you feel thankful to Allah ﷻ this week?
Which goals did you manage to concentrate on this week?
What have you discovered this week about yourself or your intentions?
What do you plan to prioritise for the coming week?
What instances or stories of Barakah did you have this week?

NIYYAH - WEEKLY PLANNING

WEEKLY GOALS

1.
2.
3.
4.

WEEKLY TASKS

"If you are grateful, I will add more (favours) unto you."
(Quran 14:7)

THINGS I THANK ALLAH ﷻ FOR	WHAT I LEARNED

DAILY PLANNING & REFLECTION

What vital goals do you have for today?

List your top 5 priorities for today, ensuring they align with your weekly goals.

1. ______________________________
2. ______________________________
3. ______________________________
4. ______________________________
5. ______________________________

What will you make dua or offer istikharah for today?

____

____

____

____

____

Today's Reflection

____

____

____

____

____

____

____

____

DAILY PLANNING & REFLECTION

What vital goals do you have for today?

List your top 5 priorities for today,
ensuring they align with your weekly goals.

1. __________
2. __________
3. __________
4. __________
5. __________

What will you make dua or offer istikharah for today?

Today's Reflection

DAILY PLANNING & REFLECTION

What vital goals do you have for today?

List your top 5 priorities for today, ensuring they align with your weekly goals.

1. ________________________________
2. ________________________________
3. ________________________________
4. ________________________________
5. ________________________________

What will you make dua or offer istikharah for today?

Today's Reflection

DAILY PLANNING & REFLECTION

What vital goals do you have for today?

List your top 5 priorities for today, ensuring they align with your weekly goals.

1. ____________________
2. ____________________
3. ____________________
4. ____________________
5. ____________________

What will you make dua or offer istikharah for today?

Today's Reflection

DAILY PLANNING & REFLECTION

What vital goals do you have for today?

List your top 5 priorities for today, ensuring they align with your weekly goals.

1. ______________________________
2. ______________________________
3. ______________________________
4. ______________________________
5. ______________________________

What will you make dua or offer istikharah for today?

____

____

____

____

____

Today's Reflection

____

____

____

____

____

____

____

____

DAILY PLANNING & REFLECTION

What vital goals do you have for today?

List your top 5 priorities for today, ensuring they align with your weekly goals.

1. ________________________________
2. ________________________________
3. ________________________________
4. ________________________________
5. ________________________________

What will you make dua or offer istikharah for today?

Today's Reflection

DAILY PLANNING & REFLECTION

What vital goals do you have for today?

List your top 5 priorities for today, ensuring they align with your weekly goals.

1. ______
2. ______
3. ______
4. ______
5. ______

What will you make dua or offer istikharah for today?

______

Today's Reflection

______

MUHASABA - WEEKLY REVIEW

For what do you feel thankful to Allah ﷻ this week?

Which goals did you manage to concentrate on this week?

What have you discovered this week about yourself or your intentions?

What do you plan to prioritise for the coming week?

What instances or stories of Barakah did you have this week?

NIYYAH - WEEKLY PLANNING

WEEKLY GOALS

1.
2.
3.
4.

WEEKLY TASKS

"If you are grateful, I will add more (favours) unto you."
(Quran 14:7)

THINGS I THANK ALLAH ﷻ FOR	WHAT I LEARNED

DAILY PLANNING & REFLECTION

What vital goals do you have for today?

List your top 5 priorities for today, ensuring they align with your weekly goals.

1. ______________________________
2. ______________________________
3. ______________________________
4. ______________________________
5. ______________________________

What will you make dua or offer istikharah for today?

____

____

____

____

____

Today's Reflection

____

____

____

____

____

____

____

____

DAILY PLANNING & REFLECTION

What vital goals do you have for today?

List your top 5 priorities for today, ensuring they align with your weekly goals.

1. ______
2. ______
3. ______
4. ______
5. ______

What will you make dua or offer istikharah for today?

Today's Reflection

DAILY PLANNING & REFLECTION

What vital goals do you have for today?

List your top 5 priorities for today, ensuring they align with your weekly goals.

1. ______
2. ______
3. ______
4. ______
5. ______

What will you make dua or offer istikharah for today?

______

______

______

______

______

Today's Reflection

______

______

______

______

______

______

______

______

DAILY PLANNING & REFLECTION

What vital goals do you have for today?

List your top 5 priorities for today, ensuring they align with your weekly goals.

1. ______
2. ______
3. ______
4. ______
5. ______

What will you make dua or offer istikharah for today?

______

______

______

______

______

Today's Reflection

______

______

______

______

______

______

______

______

DAILY PLANNING & REFLECTION

What vital goals do you have for today?

List your top 5 priorities for today,
ensuring they align with your weekly goals.

1. ____________________
2. ____________________
3. ____________________
4. ____________________
5. ____________________

What will you make dua or offer istikharah for today?

Today's Reflection

DAILY PLANNING & REFLECTION

What vital goals do you have for today?

List your top 5 priorities for today, ensuring they align with your weekly goals.

1. ____________________
2. ____________________
3. ____________________
4. ____________________
5. ____________________

What will you make dua or offer istikharah for today?

Today's Reflection

DAILY PLANNING & REFLECTION

What vital goals do you have for today?

List your top 5 priorities for today,
ensuring they align with your weekly goals.

1. ____________________
2. ____________________
3. ____________________
4. ____________________
5. ____________________

What will you make dua or offer istikharah for today?

____
____
____
____
____

Today's Reflection

____
____
____
____
____
____
____
____

MUHASABA - WEEKLY REVIEW

For what do you feel thankful to Allah ﷻ this week?
Which goals did you manage to concentrate on this week?
What have you discovered this week about yourself or your intentions?
What do you plan to prioritise for the coming week?
What instances or stories of Barakah did you have this week?

NIYYAH - WEEKLY PLANNING

WEEKLY GOALS
1.
2.
3.
4.

WEEKLY TASKS	

"If you are grateful, I will add more (favours) unto you."
(Quran 14:7)

THINGS I THANK ALLAH ﷻ FOR	WHAT I LEARNED

DAILY PLANNING & REFLECTION

What vital goals do you have for today?

List your top 5 priorities for today,
ensuring they align with your weekly goals.

1. ______________________________
2. ______________________________
3. ______________________________
4. ______________________________
5. ______________________________

What will you make dua or offer istikharah for today?

Today's Reflection

DAILY PLANNING & REFLECTION

What vital goals do you have for today?

List your top 5 priorities for today,
ensuring they align with your weekly goals.

1. ____________________
2. ____________________
3. ____________________
4. ____________________
5. ____________________

What will you make dua or offer istikharah for today?

Today's Reflection

DAILY PLANNING & REFLECTION

What vital goals do you have for today?

List your top 5 priorities for today, ensuring they align with your weekly goals.

1. ______
2. ______
3. ______
4. ______
5. ______

What will you make dua or offer istikharah for today?

Today's Reflection

DAILY PLANNING & REFLECTION

What vital goals do you have for today?

List your top 5 priorities for today, ensuring they align with your weekly goals.

1. ______
2. ______
3. ______
4. ______
5. ______

What will you make dua or offer istikharah for today?

Today's Reflection

DAILY PLANNING & REFLECTION

What vital goals do you have for today?

List your top 5 priorities for today, ensuring they align with your weekly goals.

1. ____________________
2. ____________________
3. ____________________
4. ____________________
5. ____________________

What will you make dua or offer istikharah for today?

Today's Reflection

DAILY PLANNING & REFLECTION

What vital goals do you have for today?

List your top 5 priorities for today, ensuring they align with your weekly goals.

1. ____________________
2. ____________________
3. ____________________
4. ____________________
5. ____________________

What will you make dua or offer istikharah for today?

____

____

____

____

____

Today's Reflection

____

____

____

____

____

____

____

____

DAILY PLANNING & REFLECTION

What vital goals do you have for today?

List your top 5 priorities for today, ensuring they align with your weekly goals.

1. ____________________
2. ____________________
3. ____________________
4. ____________________
5. ____________________

What will you make dua or offer istikharah for today?

Today's Reflection

MUHASABA - WEEKLY REVIEW

For what do you feel thankful to Allah ﷻ this week?

Which goals did you manage to concentrate on this week?

What have you discovered this week about yourself or your intentions?

What do you plan to prioritise for the coming week?

What instances or stories of Barakah did you have this week?

MUHASABA - MONTHLY REVIEW

What did I accomplish? What did I fail to accomplish?

What benefits & drawbacks have I experienced?

What challenges have I faced? What solutions could I have adopted?

What have I learnt during the last month? How can I improve?

Greet People

And when you are greeted, respond with a better greeting or at least similarly. Surely Allah is a 'vigilant' Reckoner of all things.

[TMQ Surah An-Nisa : 86]

NIYYAH - MONTHLY PLANNING

What do I hope to accomplish by the month's end? Why?

What are the benefits & drawbacks of my goals/intentions?

What must I do in order to carry out my intentions?

What challenges have I faced? How can I overcome these challenges?

NIYYAH - WEEKLY PLANNING

WEEKLY GOALS

1.
2.
3.
4.

WEEKLY TASKS

"If you are grateful, I will add more (favours) unto you."
(Quran 14:7)

THINGS I THANK ALLAH ﷻ FOR	WHAT I LEARNED

DAILY PLANNING & REFLECTION

What vital goals do you have for today?

List your top 5 priorities for today,
ensuring they align with your weekly goals.

1. ______
2. ______
3. ______
4. ______
5. ______

What will you make dua or offer istikharah for today?

______

______

______

______

______

Today's Reflection

______

______

______

______

______

______

______

______

DAILY PLANNING & REFLECTION

What vital goals do you have for today?

List your top 5 priorities for today,
ensuring they align with your weekly goals.

1. ______________________________

2. ______________________________

3. ______________________________

4. ______________________________

5. ______________________________

What will you make dua or offer istikharah for today?

____

____

____

____

____

Today's Reflection

____

____

____

____

____

____

____

____

DAILY PLANNING & REFLECTION

What vital goals do you have for today?

List your top 5 priorities for today,
ensuring they align with your weekly goals.

1. ____________________
2. ____________________
3. ____________________
4. ____________________
5. ____________________

What will you make dua or offer istikharah for today?

Today's Reflection

DAILY PLANNING & REFLECTION

What vital goals do you have for today?

List your top 5 priorities for today, ensuring they align with your weekly goals.

1. ____________________
2. ____________________
3. ____________________
4. ____________________
5. ____________________

What will you make dua or offer istikharah for today?

Today's Reflection

DAILY PLANNING & REFLECTION

What vital goals do you have for today?

List your top 5 priorities for today,
ensuring they align with your weekly goals.

1. ______________________________
2. ______________________________
3. ______________________________
4. ______________________________
5. ______________________________

What will you make dua or offer istikharah for today?

Today's Reflection

DAILY PLANNING & REFLECTION

What vital goals do you have for today?

List your top 5 priorities for today, ensuring they align with your weekly goals.

1. ______
2. ______
3. ______
4. ______
5. ______

What will you make dua or offer istikharah for today?

______

______

______

______

______

Today's Reflection

______

______

______

______

______

______

______

______

DAILY PLANNING & REFLECTION

What vital goals do you have for today?

List your top 5 priorities for today,
ensuring they align with your weekly goals.

1. ________________________________
2. ________________________________
3. ________________________________
4. ________________________________
5. ________________________________

What will you make dua or offer istikharah for today?

Today's Reflection

MUHASABA - WEEKLY REVIEW

For what do you feel thankful to Allah ﷻ this week?
Which goals did you manage to concentrate on this week?
What have you discovered this week about yourself or your intentions?
What do you plan to prioritise for the coming week?
What instances or stories of Barakah did you have this week?

NIYYAH - WEEKLY PLANNING

WEEKLY GOALS

1.
2.
3.
4.

WEEKLY TASKS

"If you are grateful, I will add more (favours) unto you."
(Quran 14:7)

THINGS I THANK ALLAH ﷻ FOR	WHAT I LEARNED

DAILY PLANNING & REFLECTION

What vital goals do you have for today?

List your top 5 priorities for today, ensuring they align with your weekly goals.

1. __________
2. __________
3. __________
4. __________
5. __________

What will you make dua or offer istikharah for today?

Today's Reflection

DAILY PLANNING & REFLECTION

What vital goals do you have for today?

List your top 5 priorities for today,
ensuring they align with your weekly goals.

1. ____________________
2. ____________________
3. ____________________
4. ____________________
5. ____________________

What will you make dua or offer istikharah for today?

Today's Reflection

DAILY PLANNING & REFLECTION

What vital goals do you have for today?

List your top 5 priorities for today, ensuring they align with your weekly goals.

1. ______________________________
2. ______________________________
3. ______________________________
4. ______________________________
5. ______________________________

What will you make dua or offer istikharah for today?

Today's Reflection

DAILY PLANNING & REFLECTION

What vital goals do you have for today?

List your top 5 priorities for today, ensuring they align with your weekly goals.

1. ______________________________
2. ______________________________
3. ______________________________
4. ______________________________
5. ______________________________

What will you make dua or offer istikharah for today?

____

____

____

____

____

Today's Reflection

____

____

____

____

____

____

____

____

DAILY PLANNING & REFLECTION

What vital goals do you have for today?

**List your top 5 priorities for today,
ensuring they align with your weekly goals.**

1. ____________________
2. ____________________
3. ____________________
4. ____________________
5. ____________________

What will you make dua or offer istikharah for today?

Today's Reflection

DAILY PLANNING & REFLECTION

What vital goals do you have for today?

List your top 5 priorities for today, ensuring they align with your weekly goals.

1. ______________________________
2. ______________________________
3. ______________________________
4. ______________________________
5. ______________________________

What will you make dua or offer istikharah for today?

____

____

____

____

____

Today's Reflection

____

____

____

____

____

____

____

____

DAILY PLANNING & REFLECTION

What vital goals do you have for today?

List your top 5 priorities for today, ensuring they align with your weekly goals.

1. ____________________
2. ____________________
3. ____________________
4. ____________________
5. ____________________

What will you make dua or offer istikharah for today?

Today's Reflection

MUHASABA - WEEKLY REVIEW

For what do you feel thankful to Allah ﷻ this week?
Which goals did you manage to concentrate on this week?
What have you discovered this week about yourself or your intentions?
What do you plan to prioritise for the coming week?
What instances or stories of Barakah did you have this week?

NIYYAH - WEEKLY PLANNING

WEEKLY GOALS
1.
2.
3.
4.

WEEKLY TASKS	

"If you are grateful, I will add more (favours) unto you."
(Quran 14:7)

THINGS I THANK ALLAH ﷻ FOR	WHAT I LEARNED

DAILY PLANNING & REFLECTION

What vital goals do you have for today?

List your top 5 priorities for today, ensuring they align with your weekly goals.

1. ____________________
2. ____________________
3. ____________________
4. ____________________
5. ____________________

What will you make dua or offer istikharah for today?

Today's Reflection

DAILY PLANNING & REFLECTION

What vital goals do you have for today?

List your top 5 priorities for today, ensuring they align with your weekly goals.

1. ____________________
2. ____________________
3. ____________________
4. ____________________
5. ____________________

What will you make dua or offer istikharah for today?

Today's Reflection

DAILY PLANNING & REFLECTION

What vital goals do you have for today?

List your top 5 priorities for today, ensuring they align with your weekly goals.

1. ____________________
2. ____________________
3. ____________________
4. ____________________
5. ____________________

What will you make dua or offer istikharah for today?

Today's Reflection

DAILY PLANNING & REFLECTION

What vital goals do you have for today?

List your top 5 priorities for today, ensuring they align with your weekly goals.

1. ______________________________
2. ______________________________
3. ______________________________
4. ______________________________
5. ______________________________

What will you make dua or offer istikharah for today?

____

____

____

____

____

Today's Reflection

____

____

____

____

____

____

____

____

DAILY PLANNING & REFLECTION

What vital goals do you have for today?

List your top 5 priorities for today,
ensuring they align with your weekly goals.

1. ____________________
2. ____________________
3. ____________________
4. ____________________
5. ____________________

What will you make dua or offer istikharah for today?

____

____

____

____

____

Today's Reflection

____

____

____

____

____

____

____

____

DAILY PLANNING & REFLECTION

What vital goals do you have for today?

List your top 5 priorities for today, ensuring they align with your weekly goals.

1. ______________________________
2. ______________________________
3. ______________________________
4. ______________________________
5. ______________________________

What will you make dua or offer istikharah for today?

____

____

____

____

____

Today's Reflection

____

____

____

____

____

____

____

____

DAILY PLANNING & REFLECTION

What vital goals do you have for today?

List your top 5 priorities for today,
ensuring they align with your weekly goals.

1. ____________________
2. ____________________
3. ____________________
4. ____________________
5. ____________________

What will you make dua or offer istikharah for today?

Today's Reflection

MUHASABA - WEEKLY REVIEW

For what do you feel thankful to Allah ﷻ this week?

Which goals did you manage to concentrate on this week?

What have you discovered this week about yourself or your intentions?

What do you plan to prioritise for the coming week?

What instances or stories of Barakah did you have this week?

NIYYAH - WEEKLY PLANNING

WEEKLY GOALS

1.
2.
3.
4.

WEEKLY TASKS

"If you are grateful, I will add more (favours) unto you."
(Quran 14:7)

THINGS I THANK ALLAH ﷻ FOR	WHAT I LEARNED

DAILY PLANNING & REFLECTION

What vital goals do you have for today?

List your top 5 priorities for today, ensuring they align with your weekly goals.

1. ________________________________
2. ________________________________
3. ________________________________
4. ________________________________
5. ________________________________

What will you make dua or offer istikharah for today?

Today's Reflection

DAILY PLANNING & REFLECTION

What vital goals do you have for today?

List your top 5 priorities for today, ensuring they align with your weekly goals.

1. ____________________
2. ____________________
3. ____________________
4. ____________________
5. ____________________

What will you make dua or offer istikharah for today?

Today's Reflection

DAILY PLANNING & REFLECTION

What vital goals do you have for today?

List your top 5 priorities for today, ensuring they align with your weekly goals.

1. ____________________
2. ____________________
3. ____________________
4. ____________________
5. ____________________

What will you make dua or offer istikharah for today?

Today's Reflection

DAILY PLANNING & REFLECTION

What vital goals do you have for today?

List your top 5 priorities for today,
ensuring they align with your weekly goals.

1. ____
2. ____
3. ____
4. ____
5. ____

What will you make dua or offer istikharah for today?

Today's Reflection

DAILY PLANNING & REFLECTION

What vital goals do you have for today?

List your top 5 priorities for today, ensuring they align with your weekly goals.

1. ____________________
2. ____________________
3. ____________________
4. ____________________
5. ____________________

What will you make dua or offer istikharah for today?

Today's Reflection

DAILY PLANNING & REFLECTION

What vital goals do you have for today?

List your top 5 priorities for today,
ensuring they align with your weekly goals.

1. __________
2. __________
3. __________
4. __________
5. __________

What will you make dua or offer istikharah for today?

Today's Reflection

DAILY PLANNING & REFLECTION

What vital goals do you have for today?

List your top 5 priorities for today, ensuring they align with your weekly goals.

1. ____________________
2. ____________________
3. ____________________
4. ____________________
5. ____________________

What will you make dua or offer istikharah for today?

Today's Reflection

MUHASABA - WEEKLY REVIEW

For what do you feel thankful to Allah ﷻ this week?

Which goals did you manage to concentrate on this week?

What have you discovered this week about yourself or your intentions?

What do you plan to prioritise for the coming week?

What instances or stories of Barakah did you have this week?

MUHASABA - MONTHLY REVIEW

What did I accomplish? What did I fail to accomplish?

What benefits & drawbacks have I experienced?

What challenges have I faced? What solutions could I have adopted?

What have I learnt during the last month? How can I improve?

Seeking Knowledge

The Messenger of Allah (PBUH) said:

The virtue of knowledge is more beloved to me than the virtue of worship, and the best of your religion is piety.

[Al-Ādāb lil-Bayhaqī : 818]

NIYYAH - MONTHLY PLANNING

What do I hope to accomplish by the month's end? Why?

What are the benefits & drawbacks of my goals/intentions?

What must I do in order to carry out my intentions?

What challenges have I faced? How can I overcome these challenges?

NIYYAH - WEEKLY PLANNING

WEEKLY GOALS

1.
2.
3.
4.

WEEKLY TASKS

"If you are grateful, I will add more (favours) unto you."
(Quran 14:7)

THINGS I THANK ALLAH ﷻ FOR	WHAT I LEARNED

DAILY PLANNING & REFLECTION

What vital goals do you have for today?

List your top 5 priorities for today,
ensuring they align with your weekly goals.

1. ______________________________
2. ______________________________
3. ______________________________
4. ______________________________
5. ______________________________

What will you make dua or offer istikharah for today?

Today's Reflection

DAILY PLANNING & REFLECTION

What vital goals do you have for today?

List your top 5 priorities for today, ensuring they align with your weekly goals.

1. ____________________
2. ____________________
3. ____________________
4. ____________________
5. ____________________

What will you make dua or offer istikharah for today?

____

____

____

____

____

Today's Reflection

____

____

____

____

____

____

____

____

DAILY PLANNING & REFLECTION

What vital goals do you have for today?

List your top 5 priorities for today,
ensuring they align with your weekly goals.

1. ____________________
2. ____________________
3. ____________________
4. ____________________
5. ____________________

What will you make dua or offer istikharah for today?

Today's Reflection

DAILY PLANNING & REFLECTION

What vital goals do you have for today?

List your top 5 priorities for today, ensuring they align with your weekly goals.

1. ____________________
2. ____________________
3. ____________________
4. ____________________
5. ____________________

What will you make dua or offer istikharah for today?

Today's Reflection

DAILY PLANNING & REFLECTION

What vital goals do you have for today?

List your top 5 priorities for today, ensuring they align with your weekly goals.

1. ____

2. ____

3. ____

4. ____

5. ____

What will you make dua or offer istikharah for today?

Today's Reflection

DAILY PLANNING & REFLECTION

What vital goals do you have for today?

List your top 5 priorities for today,
ensuring they align with your weekly goals.

1. ______________________________
2. ______________________________
3. ______________________________
4. ______________________________
5. ______________________________

What will you make dua or offer istikharah for today?

Today's Reflection

DAILY PLANNING & REFLECTION

What vital goals do you have for today?

List your top 5 priorities for today,
ensuring they align with your weekly goals.

1. ____________________
2. ____________________
3. ____________________
4. ____________________
5. ____________________

What will you make dua or offer istikharah for today?

Today's Reflection

MUHASABA - WEEKLY REVIEW

For what do you feel thankful to Allah ﷻ this week?
Which goals did you manage to concentrate on this week?
What have you discovered this week about yourself or your intentions?
What do you plan to prioritise for the coming week?
What instances or stories of Barakah did you have this week?

NIYYAH - WEEKLY PLANNING

WEEKLY GOALS

1.
2.
3.
4.

WEEKLY TASKS

"If you are grateful, I will add more (favours) unto you."
(Quran 14:7)

THINGS I THANK ALLAH ﷻ FOR	WHAT I LEARNED

DAILY PLANNING & REFLECTION

What vital goals do you have for today?

List your top 5 priorities for today, ensuring they align with your weekly goals.

1. __________
2. __________
3. __________
4. __________
5. __________

What will you make dua or offer istikharah for today?

Today's Reflection

DAILY PLANNING & REFLECTION

What vital goals do you have for today?

List your top 5 priorities for today,
ensuring they align with your weekly goals.

1. ____________________
2. ____________________
3. ____________________
4. ____________________
5. ____________________

What will you make dua or offer istikharah for today?

Today's Reflection

DAILY PLANNING & REFLECTION

What vital goals do you have for today?

List your top 5 priorities for today, ensuring they align with your weekly goals.

1. ______________________________
2. ______________________________
3. ______________________________
4. ______________________________
5. ______________________________

What will you make dua or offer istikharah for today?

____

____

____

____

____

Today's Reflection

____

____

____

____

____

____

____

____

DAILY PLANNING & REFLECTION

What vital goals do you have for today?

List your top 5 priorities for today,
ensuring they align with your weekly goals.

1. ____________________
2. ____________________
3. ____________________
4. ____________________
5. ____________________

What will you make dua or offer istikharah for today?

Today's Reflection

DAILY PLANNING & REFLECTION

What vital goals do you have for today?

List your top 5 priorities for today, ensuring they align with your weekly goals.

1. ______
2. ______
3. ______
4. ______
5. ______

What will you make dua or offer istikharah for today?

______

______

______

______

______

Today's Reflection

______

______

______

______

______

______

______

______

DAILY PLANNING & REFLECTION

What vital goals do you have for today?

List your top 5 priorities for today,
ensuring they align with your weekly goals.

1. ______________________________
2. ______________________________
3. ______________________________
4. ______________________________
5. ______________________________

What will you make dua or offer istikharah for today?

Today's Reflection

DAILY PLANNING & REFLECTION

What vital goals do you have for today?

List your top 5 priorities for today, ensuring they align with your weekly goals.

1. ____________________
2. ____________________
3. ____________________
4. ____________________
5. ____________________

What will you make dua or offer istikharah for today?

Today's Reflection

MUHASABA - WEEKLY REVIEW

For what do you feel thankful to Allah ﷻ this week?

Which goals did you manage to concentrate on this week?

What have you discovered this week about yourself or your intentions?

What do you plan to prioritise for the coming week?

What instances or stories of Barakah did you have this week?

NIYYAH - WEEKLY PLANNING

WEEKLY GOALS

1.
2.
3.
4.

WEEKLY TASKS

"If you are grateful, I will add more (favours) unto you."
(Quran 14:7)

THINGS I THANK ALLAH ﷻ FOR	WHAT I LEARNED

DAILY PLANNING & REFLECTION

What vital goals do you have for today?

List your top 5 priorities for today,
ensuring they align with your weekly goals.

1. ____
2. ____
3. ____
4. ____
5. ____

What will you make dua or offer istikharah for today?

Today's Reflection

DAILY PLANNING & REFLECTION

What vital goals do you have for today?

List your top 5 priorities for today, ensuring they align with your weekly goals.

1. ____________________
2. ____________________
3. ____________________
4. ____________________
5. ____________________

What will you make dua or offer istikharah for today?

Today's Reflection

DAILY PLANNING & REFLECTION

What vital goals do you have for today?

List your top 5 priorities for today, ensuring they align with your weekly goals.

1. ______
2. ______
3. ______
4. ______
5. ______

What will you make dua or offer istikharah for today?

Today's Reflection

DAILY PLANNING & REFLECTION

What vital goals do you have for today?

List your top 5 priorities for today, ensuring they align with your weekly goals.

1. ______
2. ______
3. ______
4. ______
5. ______

What will you make dua or offer istikharah for today?

______

______

______

______

______

Today's Reflection

______

______

______

______

______

______

______

______

DAILY PLANNING & REFLECTION

What vital goals do you have for today?

List your top 5 priorities for today, ensuring they align with your weekly goals.

1. ____________________
2. ____________________
3. ____________________
4. ____________________
5. ____________________

What will you make dua or offer istikharah for today?

Today's Reflection

DAILY PLANNING & REFLECTION

What vital goals do you have for today?

List your top 5 priorities for today,
ensuring they align with your weekly goals.

1. ______
2. ______
3. ______
4. ______
5. ______

What will you make dua or offer istikharah for today?

Today's Reflection

DAILY PLANNING & REFLECTION

What vital goals do you have for today?

List your top 5 priorities for today,
ensuring they align with your weekly goals.

1. ____________________
2. ____________________
3. ____________________
4. ____________________
5. ____________________

What will you make dua or offer istikharah for today?

____

____

____

____

____

Today's Reflection

____

____

____

____

____

____

____

____

MUHASABA - WEEKLY REVIEW

For what do you feel thankful to Allah ﷻ this week?
Which goals did you manage to concentrate on this week?
What have you discovered this week about yourself or your intentions?
What do you plan to prioritise for the coming week?
What instances or stories of Barakah did you have this week?

NIYYAH - WEEKLY PLANNING

WEEKLY GOALS

1.
2.
3.
4.

WEEKLY TASKS

"If you are grateful, I will add more (favours) unto you."
(Quran 14:7)

THINGS I THANK ALLAH ﷻ FOR	WHAT I LEARNED

DAILY PLANNING & REFLECTION

What vital goals do you have for today?

List your top 5 priorities for today, ensuring they align with your weekly goals.

1. ____________________
2. ____________________
3. ____________________
4. ____________________
5. ____________________

What will you make dua or offer istikharah for today?

____

____

____

____

____

Today's Reflection

____

____

____

____

____

____

____

____

DAILY PLANNING & REFLECTION

What vital goals do you have for today?

List your top 5 priorities for today,
ensuring they align with your weekly goals.

1. ______________________________
2. ______________________________
3. ______________________________
4. ______________________________
5. ______________________________

What will you make dua or offer istikharah for today?

____
____
____
____
____

Today's Reflection

____
____
____
____
____
____
____
____

DAILY PLANNING & REFLECTION

What vital goals do you have for today?

List your top 5 priorities for today,
ensuring they align with your weekly goals.

1. ______________________________
2. ______________________________
3. ______________________________
4. ______________________________
5. ______________________________

What will you make dua or offer istikharah for today?

Today's Reflection

DAILY PLANNING & REFLECTION

What vital goals do you have for today?

List your top 5 priorities for today, ensuring they align with your weekly goals.

1. ____________________
2. ____________________
3. ____________________
4. ____________________
5. ____________________

What will you make dua or offer istikharah for today?

____

____

____

____

____

Today's Reflection

____

____

____

____

____

____

____

____

DAILY PLANNING & REFLECTION

What vital goals do you have for today?

List your top 5 priorities for today, ensuring they align with your weekly goals.

1. ________________________________
2. ________________________________
3. ________________________________
4. ________________________________
5. ________________________________

What will you make dua or offer istikharah for today?

Today's Reflection

DAILY PLANNING & REFLECTION

What vital goals do you have for today?

List your top 5 priorities for today,
ensuring they align with your weekly goals.

1. ______
2. ______
3. ______
4. ______
5. ______

What will you make dua or offer istikharah for today?

______

______

______

______

______

Today's Reflection

______

______

______

______

______

______

______

______

DAILY PLANNING & REFLECTION

What vital goals do you have for today?

List your top 5 priorities for today, ensuring they align with your weekly goals.

1. ____________________
2. ____________________
3. ____________________
4. ____________________
5. ____________________

What will you make dua or offer istikharah for today?

Today's Reflection

MUHASABA - WEEKLY REVIEW

For what do you feel thankful to Allah ﷻ this week?

Which goals did you manage to concentrate on this week?

What have you discovered this week about yourself or your intentions?

What do you plan to prioritise for the coming week?

What instances or stories of Barakah did you have this week?

MUHASABA - MONTHLY REVIEW

What did I accomplish? What did I fail to accomplish?
What benefits & drawbacks have I experienced?
What challenges have I faced? What solutions could I have adopted?
What have I learnt during the last month? How can I improve?

www.ingramcontent.com/pod-product-compliance
Lightning Source LLC
Chambersburg PA
CBHW062135160726
48282CB00027B/829
* 9 7 8 8 1 9 6 0 8 0 2 0 4 *